MICROSERVICES: PATTERNS

AND APPLICATIONS

DESIGNING FINE-GRAINED SERVICES
BY APPLYING PATTERNS

LUCAS KRAUSE

This version was published on 4-17-2015

V1.5

Get additional information, code samples
and community support at:

microservicesbook.io

FOR LIZ AND LILY

WHY I WROTE THIS BOOK

I began my own foray into Microservices many years ago and attended many conferences learning about fine-grained systems, benefits and pitfalls. As a software designer, developer and architect for many years, I believe that all architecture choices I'd made were always the most important choices effecting the outcome and the success of software creation.

Microservices is a major architectural shift and is a fundamentally different way of building software. When I started writing this book there weren't many resources except conferences and blogs. I was excited about the prospect of designing and building these systems and I wanted to share my experience with the world to aide other developers, architects, administrators and managers to better understand Microservices.

WHY YOU SHOULD READ THIS BOOK

This book is to help you understand Microservices and how you can use them to solve problems, it outlines when to use Microservices and how to think about the Microservice architecture which is a departure from traditional software design paradigms. Microservices is creating and designing fine-grained, detailed and focused services for new (or to replace existing) monolithic complex applications. Microservices adhere to a core tenet of the UNIX platform to "do one thing and do it well."

This book explains Microservice architecture, patterns, and designs and how they allow your solution to scale, be easier to change and adapt to evolving needs. This book is for software designers (Architects, Engineers, Administrators and Managers) and also for people who just want to learn more about what Microservices are and what makes them important.

FIGURES AND TABLES

Table Of Contents

CHAPTER 1. MICROSERVICES

Microservices are the next big thing in modern software architecture and development. Since the inception of the computer, building software has been a complicated and difficult process. Many challenges may seem different but are all too common in the industry and the solutions spanning generations seem to change from centralized computing (mainframes) to distributed computing (pc) back and forth with each wave of new technologies and hardware capability, adding more choices and at the same time making things more confusing.

Distributed architecture is part of a sea-change in the industry and distributed systems have massively changed the way technology works, specifically:

- Git (distributed source control).
- Cloud Computing (AWS, Google Cloud, Azure).
- Bit torrent (distributed file sharing).
- Bitcoin (distributed virtual cryptocurrencies).

These technologies have changed the way computer systems are used, work and built. The advent of Microservices is a logical evolution of these disruptive changes.

The biggest reason these services are starting to gain popularity now is the intersection of operational automation and simplicity alongside a more centralized technology skillset and stack. If you review the recent innovations in cloud computing, virtualization and container technology, it makes the operational management of Microservices easier. Many of the recent advances in technology, specifically cloud infrastructure, containers, event processing, and service buses, all lower the barriers to accomplish what would have been much more difficult with older technologies. Unified software languages, specifically JavaScript, are also a reason this makes sense. The availability of easy server-side and client-side technologies sharing the same language makes things easier to understand and also increases the rate of innovation and maturity.

WHAT ARE THEY AND WHY ARE THEY IMPORTANT?

"The Microservice architectural style is an approach to developing a single application as a suite of small services, each running in its own process and communicating with lightweight mechanisms, often an HTTP resource API. These services are built around business capabilities and independently deployable by fully automated deployment machinery. There is a bare minimum of centralized management of these services, which may be written in different programming languages and use different data storage technologies.
- (Fowler & Lewis, 2014)

Microservices are important simply because they add unique value in a way of simplification of complexity in systems. By breaking apart your system or application into many smaller parts, you show ways of reducing duplication, increasing cohesion and lowering your coupling between parts, thus making your overall system parts easier to understand, more scalable and easier to change. The downside of a distributed system is that it is always more complex from a systems standpoint. The overhead of many small services to manage is another factor to consider.

The current state of Microservices is more of an art than a science and the technology is changing rapidly. There is a tradeoff where you are trading systems complexity for the ability to change the system, scale the system and operate the system, in most cases, more cost effectively. The good news is that this systems complexity is better managed with tools and automation, which is the critical factor as to why it is gaining popularity now.

Microservice systems are straightforward and the parts are easy to understand, however designing and breaking down the logic in your system is anything but simple. It requires knowledge of the domain and business needs along with experience with the integration and interaction of the systems and parts. If you are coming from a truly monolithic application to Microservices, this is a challenge. If you already have a system using layering or a service oriented architecture, then you have a better starting point to embrace Microservices.

The primary importance of Microservices is that our system will be easy to change in an environment where requirements constantly change, saving time, resources and money. The reality is that software needs to embrace change to be more competitive, give our users what they want and gain efficiencies; all the things that matter most to business and the users of our software.

Bounded Contexts is a term used by Eric Evans in his book "Domain-Driven Design," which explains how to model and design complex software. A Bounded Context is simply a definition for the boundary of a specific requirement or responsibility.

MICROSERVICES

You could argue that Microservices are an abstraction and technology agnostic. This may be accurate, but it is not this easy. Building Microservices in any language or technology stack is possible but the maintenance and operational support for many systems would probably counter any benefit of the system design as the tooling and deployment technologies for these frameworks are large and complex. If you had a large enterprise system comprised of a dozen parts, using Microservices would expand this to up to 3 to 5 times as many services, making management and maintenance a big challenge.

Although the philosophy of Microservices is breaking down a system into many smaller parts as all services each "doing one thing well," there is more to it. These systems also have to be independently deployable by automated deployment machinery, along with a facility of centralized management. These are the keys that make this architecture operationally feasible. The maturity of Developer Operations (DevOps) has allowed the architecture of systems to evolve into a system that was not possible a decade ago.

Newer technologies like Node.js, Docker and Git enable Microservices with DevOps easily rather than older technologies like Java or C#. You can write Microservices in any language but leveraging the automation, scalability and deployment can be tricky with every language. I expect the landscape to change, making DevOps feasible for all languages and stacks, but currently the maturity for older languages is not well established.

PRINCIPLES OF MICROSERVICES

- Encapsulation
  Services should hide how they work and do a single thing and do it well. The encapsulation is based on the business function of the service that it encapsulates; the functional requirements.

- Automation

  Services should use automation which keeps management and operational support efficient. Employing large numbers of small services can become a mess if you do not embrace automation.

- Business Domain Centric

  Similar to Encapsulation, each service should align to your bounded context within a domain model for this to make sense in the domain and in the large service architecture.

- Decentralization

  Every service should be decentralized and autonomous so that each service can operate on its own schedule and priorities. Each service, if independent, can be updated and deployed as fit. Service versioning and backwards compatibility is crucial because systems will be dependent on other systems; we can implement features and prioritize services separately.

- Independence
  Services should be independent of each other but to
  enable this similar to decentralization, we must
  implement versioning and backwards compatibility.
  Being able to deploy a service separately is the main
  goal.

- Fail-Safe
  Enterprise systems typically need to be smart, in that
  they fail in a way that doesn't break things in
  unpredictable ways. Anticipate failure in everything,
  along with validation of input and validation of data
  we send downstream.

- Observable
  While having many services enables scalability and
  simplicity of interaction, to get a bigger picture, each
  service should be observable through logging and
  correlation of messages. A common pattern here is to
  aggregate data for all services and collect and analyze
  for operational support.

SCALABILITY CUBE

The book "The Art of Scalability," describes a useful three-dimensional scalability model called the "scale cube." This is a great way to understand how Microservices fits into the scalability picture.

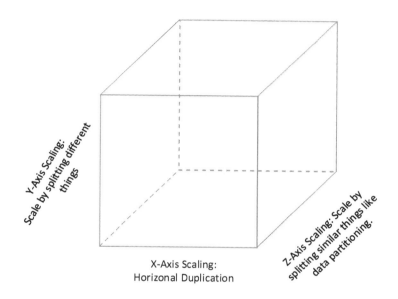

Figure 1 Scale Cube

X-Axis scaling is simply horizontal duplication. This is the typical scalability used today, having server farms and machines with a load-balancer.

Y-Axis scaling is functional decomposition which is a core principle of Microservices. This scales by splitting out different things like individual Microservices.

Z-Axis scaling is data partitioning – scale by splitting similar things, or partitioning databases, is a common usage scenario. An example of data partitioning would be a phone book with two databases A-K and L-Z. Splitting out data into two databases makes it easy. If request needs data for a person with last name starting with B, it goes to first partition, otherwise the second partition. It is generally acceptable practice for scaling very large databases.

WHEN ARE MICROSERVICES THE ANSWER

Microservices makes the most sense when the core principles of Microservices align with your business and personal principles, but the most vital principle is Bounded Context and to understand the business domain.

If you have an existing mature system where you can identify the separation of services, it makes the evolution of the solution much easier. If you are starting green field it can be a real challenge to design a system. Along these lines, it might be best to validate the business processes first then refactor to Microservices once Bounded Context and domain logic is established.

HOW TO DETERMINE THE SOLUTION

Breaking apart a system with interfaces is challenging, as well as understanding the domain model and business needs. We will elaborate on this process in Chapter 5, however the solution will evolve over time and this architecture embraces change as part of the design and intent. In many ways the process to problem solving is very similar if you are programming a large application or solving a small problem. The programming methodology is to break things down into smaller parts.

Summary

In this chapter we discussed what Microservices are and what makes it important and different from previous architectures. Microservices solves the problem of allowing for change in software in a timely and resource conservative manner. Microservices embraces many common principles developed over many years and brings them all together in a unified architecture for making development, management, and design of large complex software systems easier. In the coming chapters we will go into more details on the application of this architecture to systems while also discussing real problems and solutions.

CHAPTER 2. APPROACH TO THE PROBLEM

What is the big deal? What is the problem we want to solve? Typically we would apply a Microservice solution to the problems of a monolithic system.

The term Monolithic is referenced in the book "The Art of UNIX Programming," to describe systems that get too big. (Raymond, 2003)

What are the problems we refer to when we discuss a monolithic system?

- Interdependency – Changing one part of the system is not easy because everything must be updated at the same time. This slows things down, costing time and money.

- Scalability – You must scale everything out at once rather than just the parts that need the most improvement. This raises the costs of operations or loss of time for business which could be even more expensive.

- Security – By having everything centralized in single system, if a system is compromised, more data could be exposed versus if you used Microservices.

- Complexity – With a large single codebase the business logic and encapsulation most likely makes everything more expensive; testing, maintenance, training, etc.

How do Microservices solve these problems

Microservices adhere to principles of Encapsulation, Automation, Business Domain Centric, Isolation, Fail-Safe and Observable. These principles inherently help solve or prevent these problems, but the core fundamental nature of Microservices is that they are small and have a singular simple focus.

When problems arise there is a tendency to fix the symptom rather than to find the root-cause of the problem. With complex systems, finding the root-cause is fraught with challenges. Many complex systems can be simplified and can be broken down into composite parts enabling reusability.

Common Problems and how to identify these problems

We will dive into each of these problems and outline some of the root-cause analysis that can be performed to fix each problem.

INTERDEPENDENCY

This problem is very straightforward. If a system needs to change in a way that can impact other parts of a monolithic application in unpredictable ways, there is an opportunity to fix the behavior and create one or more Microservices to solve this challenge. Software will always have dependencies. First, we need to identify and be sure it is needed, and then move to see the options for allowing a system to have some level of functionality, even if the dependencies are not available.

SCALABILITY

When the costs to run scale are prohibitive for the business function, breaking out the subsystems that need to independently scale resolves this issue. Almost every business could leverage better scalability through composable services. This is the tenet that you only pay for what you need or use, thus saving time, money and resources.

SECURITY

Security concerns have hit a new high in our current industry with hacking, exposed data, internal threats, regulation and auditing, all pivoted on the fact that many systems are online and connected making matters worse. The problem is further compounded by the lack of investment to good security practices in the past which means our monolithic applications are most likely not as secure as they should be. When we have our interfaces clearly defined and delineated into isolated systems, implementing security becomes easier across the solution and protects data by keeping more systems less centralized. The biggest win for Microservices and security is that we need to leverage many types and levels of security which is an industry standard for security.

COMPLEXITY

Complexity is pretty easy to identify when you go to analyze a system and cannot get a straight answer on how long or how many resources are needed to accomplish a straightforward change. How long does it take to onboard a developer to support an application? How much technical debt is in the system? There are even more technical ways which not many people agree on, but cyclomatic complexity, Lines of Code and object dependencies can all indicate levels of complexity.

SOLUTIONS

Through the application of Microservices, these problems can be solved. The very architecture and tenets of this system make solving these problems much more straightforward. Understanding the principles is easy but the execution on the principles is hard. Just like a successful weight-loss story or living a healthy lifestyle, many things are simple in theory but difficult in practice and executing on all of the principles of Microservices takes dedication and perseverance.

MICROSERVICE STRATEGIES

Strategies for applying Microservices are tied to the principles discussed previously but outlined in summary here:

- Value encapsulation of a business domain within each service.
- Isolation of services around interfaces (external) and shared data access.
- Leverage patterns and use patterns as a language for value to the teams.
- Align culture to the principles of Microservices.

INTERDEPENDENCY

To solve this problem, use a Domain-Driven Design approach to discovery of the Bounded Contexts and interfaces. The goal is to design the Microservices around these interfaces and approach the problem that if there is a dependency we need to see if there are options to allow a system to be read-only or alert downstream systems of older data or possibly disable only the features that are impacted by a critical dependency.

If a system is critically dependent on another system, look to combine them into a single service. Or see if you can duplicate some of the logic enough to not require a critical dependency. It really depends on the specifics, but duplicate in the name of scalability, and independence might be a tradeoff worth making. Many times if you can duplicate some parts of a system, the problem may be simplified further using a different technology that aligns more with the purpose of the software component being written. For example, say you have an ecommerce system where currently the monolithic checkout system needs to validate each product added to a shopping cart. Breaking these out the checkout has a critical dependency on the product catalog. This makes sense. But to solve this dependency we can, if a product system is down, use a cached copy or read-only copy. Another option is not to validate in checkout pipeline but wait until the order is placed (or order placement is started).

SCALABILITY

Scalability is very straightforward if we use containers or cloud infrastructure and build up Microservices as we saw in the Scale-Cube. Once isolated and deployable services are created, scaling them is a matter of using cloud technology to ramp up the service instances to meet the demand.

There is auto-scaling on some platforms, while if you have a predictable load, you can schedule resources available to save time and money. The whole goal of the Microservice architecture is that they are small, focused and can be scaled.

It is worth noting that you don't really have to use a cloud platform but it makes things a lot easier. Running your own servers in a datacenter, hosting your services as daemons, and using a load balancer takes some work. But there are some free frameworks making this easier, too. Services are pretty straightforward to host and balance load to, but in the long run the cost is not enough to justify not using cloud. That being said, there are some private cloud capabilities that can be leveraged if the data cannot be hosted in a public cloud for regulatory reasons or business needs.

Databases provide a challenge. Depending on the data needs, different platforms have different solutions. Usually a small percentage of systems actually need scalable database back-ends, utilizing CQRS pattern. Queues or Event buses can remove the need for large-scale scalable databases. If you need one, you can always use it, but there are other ways to solve these problems, which I address in Chapter 7

SECURITY

Microservices are not inherently more secure than a Monolithic application, however you have more opportunity to make them more secure. Each Microservice needs to implement its own security based on business needs and the problem space. We dive into more details, but the general approach is that by having many more services you can have more control over the security of the systems. However this can backfire and make everything less secure, especially depending on the stack and needs for security.

A general principle that has guided me well is if you don't need to store it, don't store it. Try to find creative ways of avoiding the need for security, as avoiding the risk is an ideal solution. Try to use standard libraries and generally accepted approaches and patterns. Do not implement your own encryption or security method; it is fraught with problems.

We do not want to have a centralized and dependent security system as this defeats the purpose of the Microservice distributed architecture. It is generally acceptable to use tokens, claims, API keys and things like this within each service where the data and the methods are owned by each service, but they can share the same library. It is like duplicated code, but ownership is within each service. Development of a shareable module in Node JS or a NuGet package in .NET is a common approach to code-reuse without the pitfalls of manually duplicating code.

COMPLEXITY

I wish I had the solution for all complexity in software systems. At its core, we deal with this problem by breaking things down and encapsulation of the problems to the point where the needed complexity is isolated and can be understood at a basic level.

While Microservices deals with business logic complexity and single-system monolithic complexity, it is important to note that Microservices adds its own healthy dose of complexity.

- Distributed services are complex in nature as there is movement; the more you have, the more complex things get.
- Event based systems, or CQRS based systems, are more complex than standard procedural style code. These patterns add complexity similar to the way MVC is complex but makes things easier once you understand the pattern. New things can be difficult but get better with exposure and age.
- Asynchronous systems are inherently more complex because of callbacks and multi-threading. Advances in languages and frameworks are making this less of a problem.
- Deployment and Operational Management of many services is more complex than a single large system, however using tooling this is less of a problem.

With these more system level complexities, it is no wonder why Microservices has not taken off till recently. The good news is that most of these are systemic to our industry and the general engineering practice, and over time these complexities go away.

As Microservices become more mainstream there will be more open-source and commercial solutions making it a win-win and most of these concerns will be a non-issue.

SUMMARY

In this chapter we discussed how to approach problems, how to identify problems, and more importantly, strategies on solving problems. Identifying problems is critical to understanding Microservices and solutions using Microservices. There is no easy answer, but changing your mindset and thinking of ways to get around many of the problems is a common theme here. In the next chapter we dive into the philosophy of Microservices and how the way we think of things is a reflection of how we work and what we ultimately produce.

CHAPTER 3. APPLIED MICROSERVICES MORE THAN A CHOICE, A PHILOSOPHY

Eusociality is the highest level of organization of animal sociality, exhibited by ants, bees, termites and wasps. These organisms have evolved to build colonies making them better than the sum of their parts. What these species have developed is a way to separate work out into specialized services and separation of concerns. By breaking down a complex system into smaller more manageable, clearly defined interfaces and interactions, you build a system that is more robust and scalable, similar to the way ants or bees build and run a colony.

The UNIX Philosophy originated by Ken Thomas is a set of cultural values and approaches to developing small yet capable software. The Unix Philosophy emphasizes short, simple, clear, modular and extensible code easily maintained and repurposed by developers other than its creators. The power of this is what has made UNIX so popular and no one can argue with these values, the outcome they propose, and the reality that it works.

MICROSERVICE PHILOSOPHY

The principles in Chapter 1 and 2, lay the groundwork for the core of the philosophy of Microservices which is simply based on reducing business function complexity by breaking a complex problem down into fine-grained, focused services. This philosophy is also about understanding that less is more, and more singular focus is better than trying to do two things at once.

Most materials on how to build successful software or businesses is keeping focused on a single thing. It breaks down the distraction and noise and elevates one's thoughts to a more focused purposeful intentional process. Albert Einstein said this of simplicity:

> Everything should be made as simple as possible, but not simpler. (Einstein, 1933)

EMERGENCE

How did Microservices come about? With the advent of Service Oriented Architecture (SOA) in the past decade, the ideas of SOA were espoused and promoted for all development. There has not been any wide-spread success for SOA because it was too generic and at the time was caught up in implementation details of protocols (SOAP, RPC and XML), governance and standardization.

You can look at Microservices as an emergence from SOA, or an implementation of SOA but much more clearly defined and proven to remove the baggage SOA had.

Here are the principles of SOA. You can see how they align with Microservices at many levels, but the level of abstraction was too high:

- Standardized Contracts
- Service Loose Coupling
- Service Abstraction
- Service Reusability
- Service Autonomy
- Service Statelessness
- Service Discoverability
- Service Composability

You will notice a lot of similarity, however the breakdown for Microservices is around Bounded Contextual boundaries, encapsulation, decentralization and automation. Microservices is loosely based on SOA design principles but goes further and is a logical emergence from SOA.

FAILURE

A core philosophy of Microservices is failure. It is typically not good to promote failure as a feature, but Microservices embraces failure as a first-class citizen. Our systems will fail; it is inevitable. What we can do to ensure success is to embrace this fact by implementing fail-fast approaches in our systems and degrade features and services based on known failures. In the case of the CAP (consistency, availability, partitioning) Theorem, also known as Brewer's theorem, you can have either consistency or availability with partitioning. This is why failure and inconsistencies are important.

Designing a system with failure in mind is important and it is surprising how the worst fears from edge cases and boundary conditions can be dealt with using appropriate design or having to make compromises.

EVOLUTION

Evolution as a process is a big deal and is one of the reasons why we can implement Microservices without too much risk. I have seen the approach of using Microservices when temporary or season changes are needed by businesses. It can evolve your technology teams and user comfort with the tools and processes while also delivering value in a low-risk environment.

If you have a money-generating monolithic application, want to extend some features and add new enhancements, evolving to Microservices can be beneficial in education, showcasing quick-wins, and lowering long-term risk. It is surprising how useful and practical these approaches are to making successful services.

PLATFORM AS A SERVICE (PAAS)

Platforms as a service has been a trend as a commoditization of computer hardware and operations. The advent of PaaS and the maturity of the cloud platforms has enabled businesses to make technology and implementation more cost effective.

AMAZON WEB SERVICES (AWS)

AWS is a pioneer in cloud services leading and innovating the industry. There are many more platforms, but Amazon was the first and is an industry leader.

HEROKU

Heroku is a popular PaaS as well, and was founded to deploy cloud applications. Heroku also has defined practices for cloud based Heroku apps known as the twelve factor.

Root-Cause Analysis

A common trait aligned with the principles and philosophy of Microservices is known as root-cause analysis. This is an engineering tactic to identify the core problem and fix the problem rather than fixing the symptoms. "Five Whys" is a technique developed by Sakichi Toyoda of the Toyota Motor Corporation. When you ask "why" five times, generally you can get to the root cause of a problem, and once identified, you improve holistically the entire organization and the system in which you are operating. You should leverage the "Five Whys" to solve any problems you may have adopting the principles and philosophy of Microservices.

The "Five Whys" can also be used for identifying any problem not just philosophical or principle-based problems. Philosophical problems are the hardest to get the root cause and are often caused by culture and historical inertia.

Summary

In this chapter we discussed the history and emergence of Microservices. We also explained about Microservices and the cultural context and foundations in UNIX. Microservices is a sea-change in our industry and will keep evolving and growing to solve our problems. The philosophy will not change but the implementation details most likely will. These are exciting times to be a software engineer.

CHAPTER 4. WALKTHROUGH THE PROCESS MONOLITHIC APP TO MICROSERVICE

We will start by giving a common Monolithic application example and show that moving to Microservices can add real value, in this case, improved search speed alongside with scalability for the order system. The system is an ecommerce monolithic application.

Ecommerce Monolithic Application -

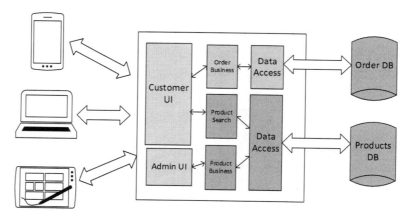

Figure 2 Monolithic Ecommerce Application

Here is an example of a monolithic ecommerce application. As you can see, there is a website showing data from product database and orders stored in an order database. Business logic and data access logic are all wrapped within the application. Managing this type of system can have some drawbacks in the complexity, dependencies and vendor lock-

36

in, all resulting in lost opportunity, lost customers and lost money.

The key to making this work in your organization and project is to do it in small increments, proving the process as you go along in an agile way. Having risk assessments evaluate the value of each component, work with the client to prioritize and make smart goals and milestones.

For this particular system the client wanted to break apart the products system from the ordering system improving product search speed, but also to allow cost effective scaling on the ordering system.

BREAKING OUT BOUNDED CONTEXTS

For this example it makes the most sense to see how to break apart products components from the orders components in respect from Bounded Context. This is a straightforward example showing the thinking process and what the perspective from the client and our teams needs to be.

After examination of the existing architecture, it is clear that the administration of the product catalog and the display of the product information should be two separate activities. The ecommerce system simply shows products and prices for customers to purchase and order. The ecommerce system does not need to update the product system; it is more of a read-only system. To scale the order system it is important to break this out as its own Microservice.

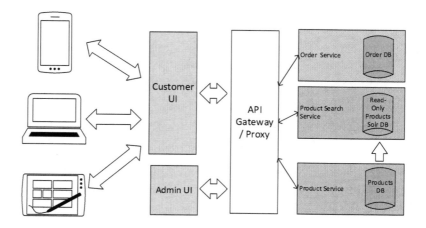

Figure 3 Microservices Ecommerce Application

The UI components and services have been broken out into separate services routed through an API Gateway / Proxy. The product service, product search and order services have been separated out. The next step is to scale out the order service. Each service is designed to be isolated, stateless, and own its own data. We can share a database between order services and scale them out to meet the load. We will get into more involved scenarios in meeting different needs based on different priorities and needs.

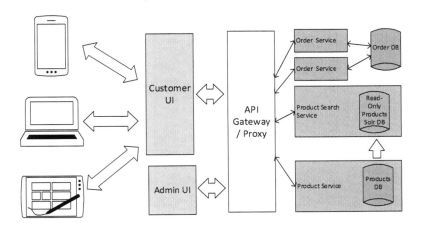

Figure 4 Microservices Ecommerce Application order service

This is an example of what a Microservice architecture looks like coming from a Monolithic application to Microservices.

One last example in this scenario is service to service communication. We remove the product search and add in the inventory services to make a point. Inventory was originally outside the monolithic app and in this case we are showing it as another Microservice. Here you can see that the order system must validate product data before it finalizes the order. Here, a valid scenario is to confirm inventory for a product placed in the order system from both the Inventory and fulfillment service along with the product service.

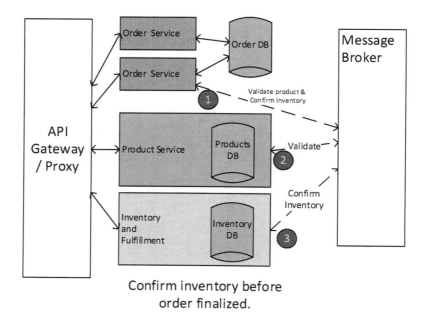

Confirm inventory before
order finalized.

Figure 5 Microservices Ecommerce Application Message Broker

The last step is that once an order has been validated, we
need to update the inventory system so it reserves product
for future orders. Ordered Messages is important here as it
removes the need for transactions between order validation
and order finalization. Once inventory is updated, inventory
system updates product if inventory is out of stock, so that
products do not show up as available in the UI.

40

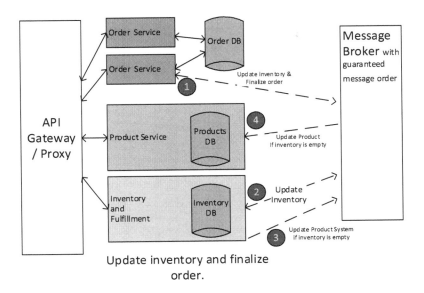

Update inventory and finalize order.

Figure 6 Microservices Ecommerce Application Finalize Workflow

This is the evolution from Monolithic application to a Microservices architecture using messaging and API Gateway for service routing and service-to-service communication. If the system can be designed so that you do both the read and update within the same message context, you can avoid some complexity. Having asynchronous processes here and ordered messages prioritized would allow the system to behave correctly. First message to check inventory and process, then the following message to update inventory to not allow orders for items that are not in stock.

ANOTHER APPROACH TO THE PROBLEM

At this point in the exercise you can clearly see that we broke out a Monolithic app into services. This is similar to Service Oriented Architecture (SOA) and Microservices and SOA. It

41

helps to think of Microservices as SOA without the baggage. If you have been in this industry in the last decade, you will remember SOA and the promises it provided. One problem is the term SOA is loaded, so unfortunately we have to rename our approach from SOA to fine-grained, decoupled, isolated, deployable, and scalable services. The key is there is no third-party baggage for Microservices. One could make the argument that SOA was not the ideal way to scale, version, or manage services. It was overly complicated and the software technology landscape was not as mature and friendly to Twelve-Factor based, cloud based service architectures.

To outline a nuance that could be overlooked in the previous section, this time we will start with a Monolith. However this time, based on our client needs and priority, the needs are different than simply scaling orders or breaking out product search.

Starting point:

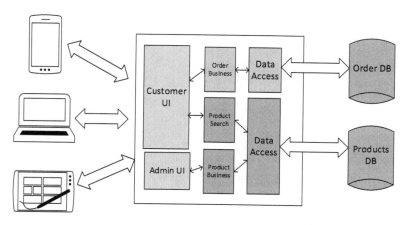

Figure 7 Monolithic Ecommerce Application

Client needs:

- A way to scale out and enhance constantly changing order history method of the order system.

New design for the priority needs of client in a different perspective. Here, we are not isolating out the order system or product systems; we are just bringing out a single part of the order system (Order History).

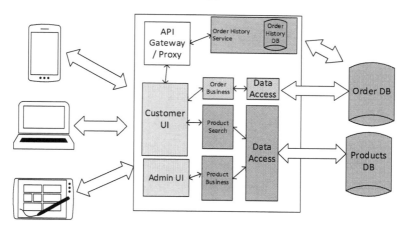

Figure 8 Microservices Ecommerce Application Breakout Order History

This design is taking a small part of the system somewhat unique and breaking it out into its own service. Using client priorities and logical boundaries is where Microservices really shines. Here we can model the Order history DB into a relational, document, Key-value or graph; any database(s) that makes sense for the problem and that would be needed to support the function of the service.

START SMALL, INCREMENTAL IMPROVEMENTS

The best way to start out on the Microservice implementations from a Monolithic Application is to start small. Find a straightforward part of the application that makes sense to break out, either a part that is rapidly changing or a part that could benefit most from scalability improvements.

We went over using a Message Broker for routing ordered messages from service-to-service for integration. In some cases you will need to interface with the Monolithic app. Some kind of stub or integration code may need to be written, depending on the complexity and functions of the Monolithic app.

We don't have to rewrite the entire app or break off a huge part. Taking a specific operation or two within a service can also make sense. The choices here really depend on the context, needs, priority, team structure, code structure, etc. Another interesting point is the order history could be written in any technology stack with any database technology, as it is all abstracted out from the monolithic application.

SUMMARY

In this chapter we walked through the process of starting from a Monolithic App and breaking it out into Microservice architecture. SOA was discussed and how similar it is to Microservices but with slightly different goals and baggage. Microservices is not clearly defined to a specific size; it is all based on the business unit of work size.

CHAPTER 5. WALKTHROUGH THE PROCESS SOA APPLICATION TO MICROSERVICE

We will start by giving a common Service Oriented Architecture (SOA) application example and show that moving to Microservices can add value in more fine-grained and defined services. The system is an Ecommerce SOA application.

Ecommerce SOA Application -

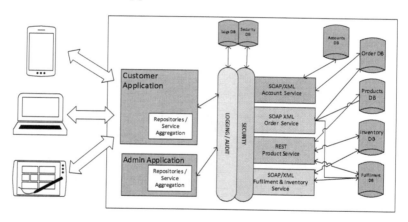

Figure 9 SOA Ecommerce Application

Here is an example of an SOA ecommerce application. As you can see a lot of the systems are broken out by feature set like accounts, orders, products and fulfillment. The system has cross-cutting concerns like logging and security. In many cases databases are shared between services, not always but more common than not. Typically, these systems are also centered on a vendor specific middleware, which is not specified here, but with this comes a lot of overhead and vendor lock-in. The downsides with this are similar to the Monolithic App. You could almost call this a monolithic SOA. This is not the recommended SOA architecture but is a realistic example of how SOA has been implemented and shows where a Microservices approach can help.

What will not help here is just replacing each service with smaller services. Usually teams, pillars, and organizational structure are reflected in these systems so that will need to be fixed as well. Here we will examine how to evolve a SOA platform to Microservices. In one way this is easier since a lot of business function is isolated and service-oriented. However, there is a lot of baggage, overhead, and dependencies plus the system gives off a sense of how services has failed and begs the question, How will Microservices help?

We approach this system in a very similar manner to the Monolithic App but taking care to learn from the organizational mistakes leading to failed SOA or at least what problems this system has. The common denominator between Monolithic App and a SOA system is the cost to maintain, and change is far too high when things can be much easier to change and prioritize.

BREAKING OUT BOUNDED CONTEXTS

Any discussion of decomposing applications into Microservices must start with the question:

"What does the client need, where is the pain, what is the context?"

For this example the client had downtime for the order services because of the product system. The client also wanted the order system to be able to operate and accept orders even if all the other services are down. The reason for the database dependencies was that for speed of development and ease of code and cooperation, the teams just accessing each other's databases was easier and more straightforward than defining interfaces and contracts between the services. SOA does not endorse sharing databases, however I have seen this as a real-world implementation of SOA after version 1.0 ships and the consultants go home. When a system survives and is versioned to the next iteration, usually version 2.0, problems with this process are referred to as the second-system effect. The system and design process degrade, the priority is on delivery and short-cuts must be made.

"The second-system effect proposes that, when an architect designs a second system, it is the most dangerous system he will ever design, because he will tend to incorporate all the additions he originated but did not add to the first system due to inherent time constraints. Thus, when embarking on a second system, an engineer should be mindful that he is susceptible to over-engineering it." (The Mythical Man-Month, 1968)

For the priority from the client we identify the order service to be refactored out of the existing SOA stack and create two unique Microservices to solve the complex problem of accepting orders and degrade service features based on availability of other systems. We can break apart order history and create order as they are unique order services on the original service while keeping the monolithic order service there, breaking things out based on priorities for the client. In this case, creating and not losing orders, degraded functionality (order history) which can be offered even if everything else is offline. The big win here is starting to break apart the data into Bounded Context and not sharing large relational databases, which is a bottle neck for the performance of the system but also makes changes more expensive. We also offer a new UI element simplified and oriented to the new services as a way to show service data give a reference architecture for future enhancements. Having the gateway as the interface for a REST API (it could be technology agnostic SOAP, TCP or REST) the specifics are not as important. Usually we implement REST as it meets the principles of modern application and API development. However for integration or specific business needs the API could be exposed using many different protocols.

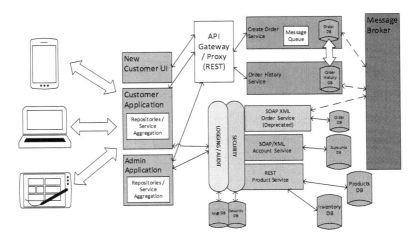

Figure 10 Microservices Ecommerce Application and Legacy SOA

The new UI component here is not critical but it is important to see that the service aggregation and orchestration moves to the API Gateway / Proxy component making clear boundaries. The applications will be lighter weight, more focused and easier to change. The next step is to add scalability to the order create service which is also using a Message Queue to ensure even if the service is down it can accept orders without issue. The larger picture is seen below along with a larger display of the order service for reference.

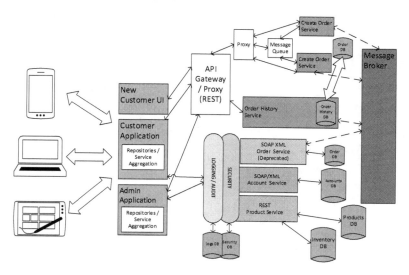

Figure 11 Microservices Ecommerce Application with Message Queue Failsafe

Depending on the needs of your services and features you have a proxy and message queue for the "create order" feature which allows orders to be processed when services become available.

Showing a higher level here, you can see the process for how orders happen in this architecture.

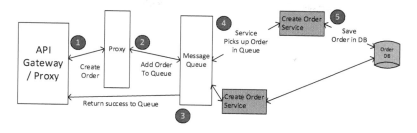

Figure 12 API Gateway with Message Queue

Step – 1 Create order comes into API, this calls proxy.

Step – 2 Proxy will add order to queue for processing.

Step – 3 Once written to Queue, return success to client.

Step – 4 Service picks up orders in the Queue.

Step -5 Order service creates order in the database.

In the case of a failure, use alerting, monitoring and management services for auto-scale. Or simply alert that a queue is filling up or that order services are down, depending on the business process needed.

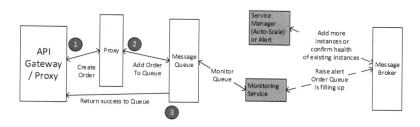

Figure 13 API Gateway with monitoring and replay

Once messages get to a queue, you are not losing any orders. A risk here is the validity of the orders and if the order service needed to do any look ups and validation, thus, the

51

quality of the orders could become an issue. Designing a system for this type of behavior is also required, it is not always just plug in some proxies and services and all is good. Analysis is needed to ensure the whole system works and supports the new architecture. Another important aspect of the design of these systems is that there are constraints which are immovable. This can make things challenging, but through clever design and following the Microservices principles, your system will succeed.

START SMALL, INCREMENTAL IMPROVEMENTS

Just like how we broke down the Monolithic Application for SOA or any large complex system, start small and incrementally build out the system. Getting client buy-in for priorities and goals changing organizational structure, team dynamics, and always striving for the core principles will make this work.

The process we are following is essentially refactoring to Microservices. This is an easier process than starting from scratch because lessons learned are in the implementation details. From the state of the current system it is clear what the problems are for the business domain, organization, teams, culture and philosophy. In Chapter 3, the philosophy and specifically root-cause analysis are tools that we have to identify and solve these problems. Typically the root-cause can be determined from adherence to the principles and philosophy of Microservices and the Microservice way of life.

SUMMARY

In this chapter we walked through the architecture from SOA to Microservices. This is a misnomer simply because

Microservices are SOA, but we need to differentiate between the two, since there is historical baggage and many lessons learned from SOA, which Microservices solved from a philosophical point of view. In addition, the advent of cloud platforms has allowed a new level and ease of integration.

We saw how to break out based on customer priorities and to start small, not simply breaking everything out in one big step, but incrementally and focused.

CHAPTER 6. WALKTHROUGH FOR CREATING GREEN FIELD MICROSERVICES

The goal of Microservices is to simplify complex systems by breaking them down into smaller fine-grained services. Building a brand new system, also known as a Green Field project, and using Microservices is not highly recommended especially if you are just starting out. Not only is your business domain most likely still being understood, but the overhead of cloud platforms, dev-ops, and Microservice distributed architecture may be too complex and heavy-handed until you know more about the business and the needs and problems in your organization and development processes.

Let's say you know the business well and the complexity of a distributed architecture is offset with a good PaaS or cloud-platform system along with a mature team that already adheres to the many principles of Microservices. For this example, we will begin with an Ecommerce application. We start by laying out the services and teams needed, along with a cadence and approach that will allow for rapid straight-forward development.

Ecommerce Bounded Context –

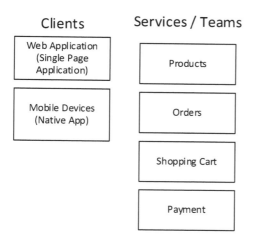

Figure 14 Domain and Bounded Contexts

Applying Microservices to this context we can see this as a high level architecture. This shows the basic functional separation of each business function, exporting the payment systems to a third party and utilization of a message broker for service-to-service integration. The User Interface is a web application single-page application (SPA) which is a modern approach to building web applications leveraging Microservices.

Ecommerce Microservice Bounded Context -

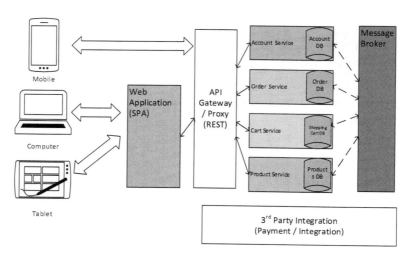

Figure 15 Green Field Microservices Architecture

BREAKING OUT BOUNDED CONTEXTS

We have Bounded Contexts with respect to the different functions of the application. The goal here is prioritization based on client needs and goals for the system. Starting in small increments, build out a lean system similar to the conceptual minimal viable product (MVP), starting with user scenarios and business cases. In this system the analysis goes along the lines of:

1. We can get away without having any account in an ecommerce system, guest check-out or not having account / login system; this is not a central requirement to the business needs.

56

2. We can also get away with not having a product database; we can stub this out with some minimal number of products or some other storage and retrieval mechanism. Obviously products and pricing can be a huge element; it is not the biggest barrier to business execution.
3. Shopping Cart is essential to an ecommerce application and should be prioritized, but the interfaces and features can be lightweight and grow based on needs.
4. Orders is a critical and centralized part of the ecommerce system; this is the final record of what is being ordered and used for calculating sales, where to ship things, receipts, and has some legal regulatory needs.
5. Payment services is critical to the ecommerce system, so this is required. However this is a third-party integration and therefore does not take much in the development and integration services.

A revised high-level architecture based on this analysis is shown below:

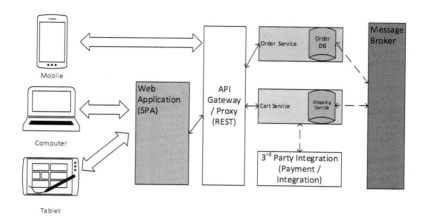

Figure 16 Green Field Microservices Architecture Breakdown into Minimal Viable Product

This is a great start to designing a green field Microservice based system, developing the MVP, and working out basic business scenarios:

1. Add/update/remove item from shopping cart.
2. View shopping cart.
3. Checkout cart / create order.
4. View order status.
5. Cancel an order.

Further breaking these out into unique services can make sense, as well as combining different use cases. Since a shopping cart is a transient process of shopping, it stands to reason that this is its own service and database. Once it has been checked out and paid for, the system will create an order from the cart, and the cart goes away. Once you have an order, payment receipt and shipping information need to be kept and tracked as part of the order procurement process.

Creating an order from a shopping cart is accomplished using a Message Broker and if high availability is needed we could leverage a Message Queue like in the previous example. Building the cart and order services as REST services makes sense and aligns with leveraging a Web SPA client using JSON as a data format.

Start Small, Incremental Improvements

Just as we broke down the Monolithic or SOA based solutions into Microservices, we are not breaking things down here but rather breaking down functionality into clearly defined fine-grained services. After the MVP has been established it would make sense to add accounts to allow users to save shopping carts, or associate customer / account details to the order, and to allow an order to be linked to a customer. Adding product-based system would not be that far-fetched, along with fulfillment and inventory management, but each of these areas needs to be tackled based on business priorities and align with the Microservice principles.

SUMMARY

In this chapter we walked through a green field ecommerce application similar to the previous two chapters, examining starting from scratch and how it is not always the most efficient process; there could be a lot of service rewriting and re-wiring in the learning process. If you know the business needs in depth and have a skilled team sharing the basic principles needed for success, then go for it. Just be aware of the tradeoffs.

CHAPTER 7. DATA

Microservices and data is a challenge for many simply because it turns the use of tried and true giant, entity-based, relational databases on its head. Each Microservice should have its own database(s) and the big win here is that with the isolation of a Microservice, we gain advantages to using the right tool for the job like using a Graph database for social data, a timeline series database for time-based analysis, or even a relational database if that is what you need for the job. One of the biggest concerns is that when you share data it has to play nice with all systems accessing the data, however with Microservices you are free from most of those compromises. Later we will discuss scenarios for sharing data or databases among services.

The playing field for data storage over the last ten years has expanded and prospered which is a win-win for everyone. You can leverage the toolset that brings the most advantages for your problem space making everything more productive and efficient. Architecture alone is one of the biggest factors for performance, security, stability and user experience for a system. Lean development methodologies postulate and show that the closer you get to the finalized and deployed system, trying to fix problems like security, scalability or performance can take an order of magnitude or more resources to resolve than if the design and starting architecture reflect and use the designs preventing these problems from existing. If we choose the right frameworks, technologies and patterns for your architecture, we can avoid many problems.

RELATIONAL DATABASES

Relational databases almost need no introduction but basically they are a cornerstone of almost every monolithic application, and usually used wherever data is needed to be persisted regardless of the actual usage scenarios. I have seen a large majority of systems using transactional and relational databases mostly as a read-only data source. The problem with relational databases is that they have expanded and added features so that they can do everything in addition to relational storage (added features like XML storage, columnar storage, advanced indexing, modular programming components), which don't really have a place in a truly data-based transactional relational system.

APPLICATIONS

Relational databases are a good way to:

- Keep normalized data which removes any data duplication.
- Transactional integrity for related data.
- Partitions and clusters with horizontal scale-out is typical pattern.
- A great model for data centric problem spaces.
- Embrace speed for transactional processing problem domains.

Relational databases are not a great choice for:

- Fast access and reporting on data.
- Documents or Hierarchical data.
- Key-Value problem spaces (caching, static data).
- Networked data (connected data like social network).

Relational databases have matured and come a long way. Performance and transactional integrity for many user cases make them common, and in a data-centric design world they make a sense. However it is important to realize our own bias when designing systems and try to look beyond the tools we know and embrace the idea that trying new things is how we evolve and get better.

No SQL

The term No SQL is not my favorite as it implies that these solutions / systems are potentially negative. The technology grew from the frustration of everything being relational even if it didn't make sense, the most common being document storage and then graph databases, time-series databases, in-memory caches, distributed databases, etc.

There are tons of different No SQL databases which exist to solve certain domain-specific problems and challenges. Since a Microservice should own its own data, leveraging these is much more straightforward from a team-perspective but also from a technology integration point of view.

APPLICATIONS

No SQL databases are varied and powerful. Examples of NO SQL database types are:

- Document databases – for storing documents or data, which is more "self-contained."
- Graph databases – represent data with a more natural relationship with other data like a social network or hierarchical data.

- Key-Value – used for high scalability and usually a key-value storage of common data or reference data or caching in memory.
- Columnar – used with large amounts of isolated data (sparse columns) for analysis systems.

FREEDOM

With Microservices now and isolated focused fine-grained systems, we can use the right tool for the right job and being encapsulated makes this a big win for simplification of the problem-space.

No SQL is mainstream and generally accepted now, however with so many varieties and solutions, the biggest challenges are finding the right fit for your problem and getting it all working together. A general software principle of doing the simplest things possible to solve the problem goes well with applying these databases to your problem space.

Risk is lowered and with the CAP theorem referenced in Chapter 3 we do not need to worry so much about ACID transactions and consistency as the nature of the systems gives us the freedom to use less robust data systems, while redundancy and eventual consistency will work for the large majority of our problems.

If your system requires ACID transactions or real-time consistency, using classic relational databases are a common solution. Transaction managers and orchestration workflows can be leveraged for these cases as well. Transaction managers and their mechanism breaks the principles of isolation and making services independently deployable, observable services, not gaining the core benefits of Microservices. I recommend breaking out parts that do not have this requirement, or work with the business to compromise to allow for eventual consistency.

Sharing Data

Sharing data is a difficult thing and gets exceptionally more difficult in a distributed architecture. There are some scenarios for shared data:

- Static reference data (countries, states, postal codes) in a database, configuration files, or source code.
- Sharing tables within a database across services.
- Sharing entire databases across services.

Strategies

To approach solving this problem we need to define the Bounded Context around the data that needs to be shared:

- Hardcode static data in code or configuration, if updated more than once a year, can leverage a key-value in memory database and keep it immutable and loaded within the services.
- Sharing tables and keeping transactions in a distributed system with performance is not possible as CAP theorem proves, so we must promote this data to its own service as a dependency. Usually it is a read-only option with the scenario wherein ensuring eventual consistency will suffice.
- Sharing databases as a whole entity is not common and should be its own service or broken out and partitioned to align better with the Bounded Context.

Summary

In this chapter we discussed Data with Microservices. We reviewed the database landscape and outlined technologies that are useful to solving specific problem spaces. Sharing of data is a challenge with any software system but and is an especially painful area with Microservices coming from Monolithic applications. In the next chapter we will go into more real world problems and challenges.

CHAPTER 8. REAL-WORLD SERVICES – PROBLEMS AND SOLUTIONS

This chapter will discuss some common real-world problems and solutions. One of the biggest problems with Microservices is the dependencies and challenges with designing services to not be all-in dependent on each other and the solutions to this. Versioning services has historically been a challenge, thus we will review techniques for successful versioning. Security is one of the biggest areas that is left until late in the development cycle and can have devastating impacts if risks and analysis are not done to ensure the problems are covered. Exception handling, logging, and time-outs are a common challenge with any system and architecture. These are critical for Microservices as they are the window into seeing how well your Microservices are behaving.

DEPENDENCY

Dependencies between Microservices is a real issue as dependencies carry risk of failure and also can impact performance and user and application experience.

There are two main approaches to aid in solving the problems with dependencies:

1. If we implement a couple patterns and gear towards degraded functionality where appropriate, we can alleviate any bad experiences and clearly see to manage the dependencies.

a. We need to implement the patterns for service registration and service discovery as this allows for dependencies to be handled and routed accordingly, essentially managing the dependencies.

b. Implement the Bulkhead-pattern with respect to trying to isolate dependency so that the service can operate in some fashion with a degraded experience (caching, failure-case, escalation or notification).

2. Implement an API Proxy with load balancing. This removes the need for service registration and discovery; it is more of a manual process through proxy configuration but I have seen it work well for simpler systems with minimal dependencies.

If a dependency is critical to a service, it would be worth reevaluating if the boundary context is really required between these services, potentially merging them or sharing the critical data through replication or mirroring.

VERSIONING

Service versioning has plagued software development, operations, and management since the dawn of our craft. There are several ways of accomplishing versioning, and to be consistent we should use Semantic Versioning, which is a standard (MAJOR.MINOR.PATCH) convention as it makes sense and is recognized everywhere.

When a MAJOR version number changes it means that the change is breaking and not backwards compatible. When a MINOR number changes it means that the change is backwards compatible. When a PATCH number changes it indicates a defect has been fixed. The approach to take in Microservices is to adhere to a couple of principles with relation to availability and not failing, or failing gracefully.

Our service should be backwards compatible where it makes sense and the easiest way to accomplish this is to keep the old version and new version of the service running side-by-side. This is the recommended scenario simply because having two independently deployed versions of code deployed in two different services adds a lot of complexity and operational pain if both code versions need to be supported in the long run. However it can also complicate things if both services can make inconsistent data. Versioning is how we support the principle of allowing teams and other services to be and to allow for different releases and deployment lifecycles.

VERSIONING TYPES

When versioning a service using semantic versioning, you can upgrade the service to a minor version and you need only to host one service and endpoint version. In the case of a breaking change, the ideal scenario is to have two endpoints of the same service on different versions. (See Figure 17) This is so the clients can upgrade when needed on their own release cycle. Once all clients have upgraded we can safely decommission the old endpoint and everything is good.

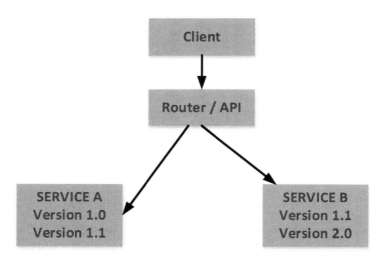

Figure 17 Versioning within the service handles logic, and when all clients are upgraded the old version can be deprecated

Another approach (Figure 18) is to host two services separately on different versions. This is really a challenge as it has much more overhead than other approaches and requires special routing to be accomplished. This is more trouble than it's worth and not recommended, but a valid option in extreme circumstances.

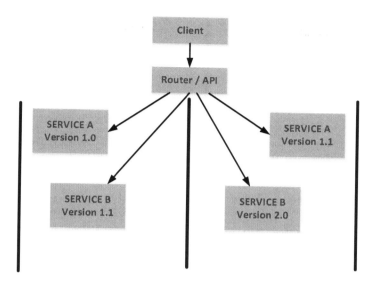

Figure 18 Service Versions side-by-side with router

VERSIONING TECHNICAL APPROACHES

Having a service we version, versioning can be implemented in several ways:

1. In the Address itself, this works well and is very common for REST web services (service/v1.2), however having version information in the name or the location of the service makes it brittle. Hardcoded versioning is common and was needed back when things were first getting starting with services and service-oriented architecture. Now there is better framework and protocol alignment to make versioning easier. Although this is common and straightforward, it is not wrong. Putting the version in the URI of an endpoint, is overkill and grounded in original SOA based isolation techniques.

2. Versioning within the message using headers, specifically content-types and accept headers to indicate the data-types and include versioning in the message routing and negotiation process. Keeping the same endpoint but expecting different message formatting can be confusing if not tested.

SECURITY

Security in this day and age is a hot-topic and doesn't get the attention it needs. Unfortunately this leads to data breaches, leaks, hacks and a lot of headaches. As far as Microservices are concerned, it is best to establish trust-boundaries as part of the domain model and each service handles its own security. It can pay off to develop what works for you and your risks, and then allow for code-reuse using modules and libraries for sharing of the security. This can be hampered if each team and service are using different technologies but you generally do not want to centralize security at the micro-service level, as this leads to a lot of overhead and failure cases which are not ideal. Using new technologies like JSON Web Tokens is a new standard that elevates the security architecture to claims-based authorization, along with techniques like API keys or TLS/SSL for tunneling of the information.

The current trend in secure systems now is to implement two-factor security and also not storing passwords at all but relying on standard common account systems using OAuth like signing on with your Google, Facebook or Twitter account.

AUTHORIZATION AND AUTHENTICATION

Authorization is checking that a person who has access to a system should be able to do the activity they are doing. Authorization is simply permissions for what you are doing like on a document; just read the document, or permission to edit.

Authentication is simply verifying the person is who they say they are. Typically, using a password or security pin ensures that the person is whom they claim to be. More recently biometrics are used to ensure a person's identity.

TWO-FACTOR AUTHENTICATION

Two-Factor authorization is having two things (instead of just one thing) the system can use to authenticate you. You need something you **know** and something you **have**. Typically this is a phone or security dongle with time-based encrypted numbers so that when you authenticate, you need to know your password but also have a device that generates a code so you have a thing and know a thing. Another less common approach is using finger-prints or a photo of a face to be the second factor.

OAUTH

Many systems have skipped storing credentials altogether and just using OAuth to link an account for a person to an identity on another open platform like Facebook, Google or Twitter. This is a real win. However, your system is taking a dependency on these external systems. It really comes down to the use cases for the system to understand if this works for your needs.

OAuth does not apply to service-to-service security. It is more of an authorization and authentication of a user to do specific functions.

API Keys

API keys have been around a long time and depending on your system requirements there are different levels in which these can be adopted. API keys give the ability for a service to control access, do fine-grained control of the client requests limiting, throttling or Quality of Service (QoS), etc.

The ways these are implemented have been standardized among the different technology stacks. The most common is a public/private key pair utilizing the gateway pattern. API Keys are much simpler to implement and leverage and are a proven and mature approach to API security.

JSON Web Tokens

JSON Web Token (JWT) is a means of representing claims to be transferred between two parties. The claims in a JWT are encoded as a JSON object that is digitally signed using JSON Web Signature (JWS) and/or encrypted using JSON Web Encryption (JWE). There is service-to-service security using tokens, similar to API keys. JWT can also be used to enforce security on a per-user basis as well. Using these two token types combined can limit what a person can do on a per-system basis. It is as flexible as you need it to be and pretty straightforward with lots of implementations across the different frameworks.

EXCEPTIONS, TIME-OUTS AND LOGGING

Designing for Exceptions, Time-Outs and Logging are vital for Microservices. This is important due to the many services, and knowing the state of the entire system is vital. Having an aggregation of error information, correlated transactions, messages, and logging of debug data is critical to high quality, as well as to aid in troubleshooting issues and having a responsive organization.

The principle that the services should be observable means having a way to get the status of a service, view the logs from a service, and viewing and dealing with exceptions through failure analysis and patterns like Circuit Breaker to aid in the fail-safe states for services.

EXCEPTIONS

Exception handling is a hot-topic in the field of engineering. Many problems have come from exceptions and their usage and use cases. The general ideal principle for exceptions is to handle them based on your business cases, but do not blindly swallow them, or catch-and-throw them, as it only adds to the inefficiencies of the system.

Ideally "less is more" and a system should never use exceptions as a happy-path use case as they are expensive and really should be exceptional not common place. When you handle, log or throw exceptions, it should be clear what the error or exception is. Most modern frameworks and languages support the idea of exception try-catch blocks and should be used to avoid the error-prone process of procedure exception handling with error codes and faults.

TIME-OUTS

Time-outs are very common in connected systems; if a system is not available, you typically get a time-out error after some threshold. When we develop Microservices it is important to use timeouts between services and systems. It is recommended to standardize on a timeout length and adjust to specific settings on a case-by-case basis.

Timeouts are most useful because they indicate if a system is behaving in an inconsistent manner. Use timeouts everywhere. They will save you time in the long run and make the system more resilient and proactive.

LOGGING

Logging is critical in Microservices. It is vital to log status, errors and timeout. It is a tried and true standard communication mechanism. Logging also enables more robustness by allowing for reply of what has happened in your service. Logging also enables better security by logging access information, auditing in some cases and troubleshooting in complicated security scenarios.

Logging is even more important when you have many services and instances running. We must use tooling to aggregate and collect all the logging data to aid in monitoring the health and reliability of our systems.

Logstash is a standard tool used for aggregation and reporting on logs in almost any format. There are several third-party commercial systems like Splunk which can do much more than log, but there are options.

Summary

In this chapter we discussed dealing with Dependencies, Versioning, Security and Exception handling and Logging. Dependencies can be dealt with using common service registration and discovery patterns, or a simple reverse proxy and refactor to registries when the systems get more complex. Versioning is a strong suit for Microservices as they should be encapsulated and isolated, thus versioning is straightforward. Security is an important topic. The approach to tokens and API keys, along with more advanced standards like JWT help keep performance high and overhead low. The key is to keep it standard. Lastly, exceptions, timeouts and logging are critically important to Microservices, as the services are autonomous and need to be monitored and the status should be observable. Logging and health monitoring are also central to Microservices.

CHAPTER 9. SCALABILITY

Scalability is the ability of a system to support various amounts of traffic and load. The modern definition is to be automated or be able to scale on-demand. The real question you need to answer first is:

"What are the requirements for your system?"

If you don't really need scalability you should not do the upfront investment in making a system scalable unless you are sure exactly what you need. The good news is that making a system scalable is not that difficult. The biggest challenges are understanding the data, dependencies and user expectations.

Scalability is really what Microservices are all about. Netflix is the poster child for Microservices in showcasing how the Microservice architecture makes sense and is a natural progression for building reliable and scalable systems, while also remaining agile, nimble and robust.

SCALE CUBE

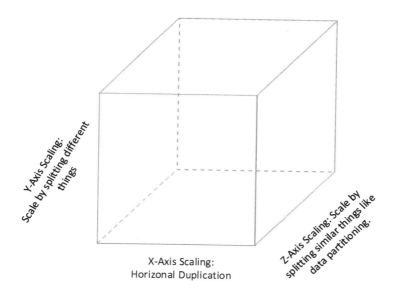

Figure 19 - Scale Cube

We learned about the scale cube in Chapter 3 and how each axis scales a system. Microservices leverage the Y-axis scalability or functional decomposition to scale out individual functions of a system as isolated services. Microservices can also scale out on X-axis as well as Z-axis, depending on the needs of a system.

CACHING

Caching is the most common denominator to scalability and performance improvement. It is also difficult to get right because many problems stem from implementing a caching strategy where cache invalidation does not occur. I have seen

79

many projects where caching was not used correctly resulting in poor performance and, worse, legal risk in charging the wrong credit cards or sending the wrong data to the wrong person.

There are three main caching-use cases: cache data at the client-side, proxy level and the server-side.

Client-Side:

We want to cache client-side to prevent network calls cutting down on traffic and load on systems. Invalidation is tricky but is possible. This is a no-brainer for making the user experience much better.

Proxy level:

Proxy caching is transparent to all systems involved. This helps cut down on network traffic and can aid in lightening the network load. Implementation of caching at the Gateway API level or Orchestrated API is where you can get more benefits than just the routing.

Server-side:

Server-side caching is really where Microservices are focused. When we can cache a service response or downstream dependency, it provides fault-tolerance but also degraded functionality in the case of an outage. I've seen server caches used heavily to abstract out an expensive database call. These are the most common forms of caches and provide many benefits with fewer problems.

CONTAINERS

Containers are the future of commoditizing application deployment and scalability. It is the most efficient way of leveraging the resources and lowering the cost of overhead. The complexity of implementing and maintaining Microservices can be mitigated by leveraging containers.

Containers work as a progressive type of virtualization wherein each container will isolate your service from other services making things more secure, predictable and supportable because of the isolation and abstraction containers provide.

The current state of containers is in its infancy. They have only been around for a couple of years and have yet to be widely adopted, but the foundation is strong and adoption is starting to take off. Some companies are starting to standardize on containers and all cloud platforms are supporting containerization as it is efficient, effective and clearly will be the future of hosted applications. Rocket from CoreOS has started development of a specification on containerization here Container Specification (http://goo.gl/EPbBsZ)

One of the biggest conceptual challenges of containers is how to manage data with containers. This is usually accomplished by using containers with networked storage. Cloud platforms have been offering this capability for several years and it is a mature approach to data management.

DOCKER

Docker is the first container to have wide-spread success. Docker is growing rapidly and I have used Docker in production systems successfully. The out of the box experience for many types of production systems is lacking and we have to implement a lot of custom tooling to make it a workable solution.

The growth and goals for Docker are aligned with supporting the more advanced orchestration and dependency problems than containers can bring. Docker is based on Linux technologies with an ultimate goal of supporting Windows, but currently, that goal is not on any roadmap. The architectural difference of Windows to Linux makes supporting both operating systems a challenge. The recent open-sourcing of Microsoft technologies make this less of an issue as you can now run native Microsoft software that is supported on Linux machines similar to the work Mono has enabled since the beginning of .NET.

Containers do not support a standard way of taking snapshots or restoring like virtual machines, however the speed with which a container can be brought online makes this less of an issue. The tradeoffs require a change in the mind-set of managing containers and virtualization in general.

ROCKET

Rocket is a new container technology created by Core OS. It is in its infancy, but focused on being lightweight and secure. Rocket was created as a response to Dockers focus more on container management and orchestration rather than just containers and container technology. Rocket brought forth a standard for the community to collaborate on and ensure that Docker does not become the de-facto standard with no competition.

Glassware 2.0

Glassware is a container technology similar to Docker and Rocket, but based on Windows software systems. It is the first container technology for Windows-based systems. Glassware is not based on any standards yet, and is a new comer to the market similar to Rocket.

Virtualization

Any discussion of scalability would not be complete without virtualization, which was the foundation of cloud platforms. The ability to virtualize operating systems has made great strides in allowing the commoditization of scaling out software as a first-generation technology. The overhead of virtual machines compared to containers is astonishing in how inefficient virtual machines are to containers. The ability to do snapshots and restores makes virtual machines support a wider variety of complex scenarios than current container technology. It is only a matter of time until containers standardize and change the way of virtualization from machine to process.

Summary

In this chapter we discussed scalability of Microservices, including the process of scalability from the Scale-Cube across the different axis along with leveraging containers and instantiation patterns to aide in the configuration and deployment of the services to scale. If you can automate deployment and configuration, you can automate scalability, which is an exciting prospect.

Chapter 10. Microservice and Monolithic Architectures

Microservice Architecture is a loaded term. It would appear to be saying "small architecture" or "making things smaller." To understand Microservice Architecture you must understand the broader and opposing architecture called Monolithic Architecture.

An application has a monolithic architecture if it has many parts contained in the application. This includes the user-interface, business libraries, database access code and usually more than one Bounded Context within the application. The term has evolved more where a monolithic app can have components broken out in layers within the application.

Scalability Problems

Monolithic systems are typically difficult to scale or only scalable horizontally, which means the whole system scales together; this is costly and an inefficient use of resources. Monolithic architectures can also scale on the Z-Axis as data partitioning as an abstraction of the data.

Monolithic Architecture

Monolithic architectures are practically everywhere; it is our current standard way of developing software systems. The common thread is that "monolithic" means big and singular;

a system that does many things and has many responsibilities. Monolithic architectures are typically difficult to deploy, difficult to upgrade and maintain and difficult to understand. (Richardson, 2014)

Monolithic architecture looks like a system that has one or two large databases, centralized functions spanning many different business needs. These systems contain presentation components, business logic, database access logic and system integration logic. The key is that these parts are spread across several different functional areas of the system.

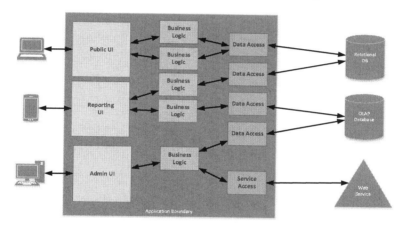

Figure 20 Monolithic Architecture

WHY IS THIS A CHALLENGE?

It is important to mention that not all monolithic systems have these problems. But the reasons systems tend to get to this point are:

- Technology changes fast – and as it changes it can make systems brittle, difficult and error prone, supporting many different changing technologies.

- Technical debt – it is common to meet a deadline to take shortcuts intentionally to get things launched. This can lead to messy interfaces, bloated code, or worst of all, critical defects.

- Change – this is the biggest cause of problems for these systems because as needs and requirements change, the system needs to change. The systems are big and any change takes a lot of time and money, even if the change is small.

- People – historically when computers were really expensive, the goal of software development was to make the programming code as efficient as possible to maximize value. Computers have gotten exponentially faster and now the opposite is true. Today the limiting factor is to optimize the efficiency of the person programming the system. Having a big monolithic system is inefficient as it takes people longer to understand and to maintain.

With these common forces in the industry you can clearly see why new patterns and techniques are emerging to overcome these challenges.

MICROSERVICES ARCHITECTURE

A Microservices Architecture comes from applying a Y-axis scaling and functionally decomposing the business functions into a set of collaborating services. Each service should implement a collection of small and related functions usually at a bounded context. (Richardson, 2014)

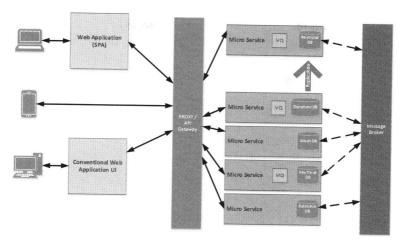

Figure 21 Microservice Architecture

Microservices are developed and deployed independently of each other and each has its own database to be decoupled. If sharing data is necessary, replication, eventing can synchronize the systems or leverage eventual consistency depending on the business needs.

Benefits:

- Easier to understand each service and functional requirements.
- Faster to deploy, because each service is independent.
- Easier to test as the functions are more isolated and decoupled.
- Easier and cheaper to scale – what needs to be scaled can be scaled independently.
- Technology-stack agnostic - you can develop each service using whatever technologies make the most sense and avoid stack lock-in.

- Improved fault isolation - a single service issue does not impact other services like a monolithic system.

Drawbacks:

- Distributed systems are more complex than a single centralized system.
- System testing can be more difficult having to test more surface area.
- Having a single scenario spread across multiple services is a challenging problem without using distributed transactions.
- Deployment and Operational complexity – having many different systems is tricky without automation and tooling, especially if each service uses vastly different technology stacks.
- If not using containers, the memory needs are much larger than a single monolithic application.

WHEN TO APPLY CHALLENGE

The biggest issue with this architecture is when to use it. On the first version of a system being developed you usually do not have the problems that this architecture resolves. Using a more complicated distributed architecture for a simple conceptual application is counter-intuitive to getting an idea out for business validation. The counter-point for this would be if you developed a monolithic system and then tried to detangle the dependencies and decompose it into a set of services. This could be even more daunting and difficult.

A common problem besides the catch-22 of how to start development with Microservices is how to partition out the system into services, because you can decompose into too small of services, what is commonly referred to as nano-services. There are some approaches to decomposition below:

- Partition services by verb or use-case.
  - Business scenarios.
  - An example is in ecommerce; you have fulfillment, or payment as separate services.
- Partition services by noun or resources.
  - Divide out by resource type per service.
  - Example is a user or account-service that operates on a user of a system.

The core philosophy of Microservices is to respect the Single Responsible Principle (SRP) which means a service should only have a single reason to change, a single responsibility. This also aligns with the philosophy of UNIX utilities, which simply do one thing and do it well.

SOLVING COMPLEXITY OF DISTRIBUTED SYSTEMS

The core complexity of Microservices is the interaction of the services and context. You can leverage a Message Broker architecture with an API Gateway to resolve a lot of this complexity. There are a few standard and open-source solutions to these problems and embracing event-based messaging is a key reason why Microservices are currently feasible and make them friendlier.

SUMMARY

In this Chapter we discussed the Monolithic and Microservices Architectures. Monolithic is centralized and brittle, slow to change and hard and expensive to change and scale. Microservices are more complex as a system, but the system allows for easier scalability, maintenance and more productive teams.

CHAPTER 11. MICROSERVICE PATTERNS

Christopher Alexander a renowned architect and author wrote many seminal architectural books, including "The Timeless Way of Building" and "A Pattern Language: Towns, Buildings, Construction." These books are the foundation for the purpose and use of patterns as a language and tool for maturing the design and understanding of systems. While Christopher Alexander is a physical building architect, the similarities between constructing buildings and constructing software systems are many:

- Complexity needs to be managed.
- Communication is critical for success.
- Industry adoption of standards and terminology.

What Christopher Alexander found was using patterns as a language to describe how to identify if a pattern applies and what the outcome should be. It is important to note that a pattern is not a recipe. This is a tough concept to come to terms with. Patterns are not simply a cookbook, but a way of thinking about a problem and a solution. When you offer an implementation with a pattern, it is a dangerous line, as many people mistakenly think this is the pattern rather than a single expression of that pattern, which can be applied using any technology or methodology, as long as it applies to the problem and solves the problem.

The patterns in this chapter deal with the Microservice ecosystem; how to call into services, registration, discovery, instantiation and systems integration. For most large and complex systems using these patterns takes some effort, but only apply what is needed and makes sense.

CHALLENGES

Some challenges with these patterns are that they are heavy-handed for simple scenarios. But when the inevitable complexity in dependencies comes, these patterns can help solve the problem. If you are committed to a cloud platform, know that most platforms offer many alternatives to manually implementing all of these patterns.

ALTERNATIVES TO THE PATTERNS

Rather than use a discovery and registration pattern, the API Gateway can use a content delivery network with load balancers and reverse proxy so you don't need to use a service repository or registration and discovery. Services would be hard-coded in the CDN / Load Balancers and reverse proxies making maintenance more difficult. If things change, the system can take time to configure and update, so there is a risk of downtime. Hardcoding services and routing is a common and simple approach, which cloud infrastructure makes easier, but locks you into the vendor.

If we have service-to-service dependency then you would have a CDN / reserves proxy for each isolated service(s) as appropriate, making things really flexible. That being said, using a service registry and using discovery is powerful and makes long-term management easier. It is just a barrier to getting things off the ground and has not proved to work well for historical service oriented systems. The big challenge is that either way there is maintenance of a service registry and discovery system, but the management is more centralized.

Below the patterns for Microservices are broken into several categories:

1. API Patterns

API PATTERNS

These patterns show how to expose services to client systems; rich-client, mobile or other services.

API PROXY PATTERN

The API Proxy is simple: allowing an API to support many different user-types of the API as first-class citizens. What this means is that your needs may support:

- Native mobile clients
- HTML 5 browsers

Each of these could expect different types of data, different load and scalability needs and different service collections. If we examine an ecommerce system, you would have a web application that exposes and allows for browsing and purchasing items, reviews, order history and pricing data.

The problem is that for each client type you can have different versions or types of services and dependencies needed to support the user scenarios. How do clients of Microservices access the individual services?

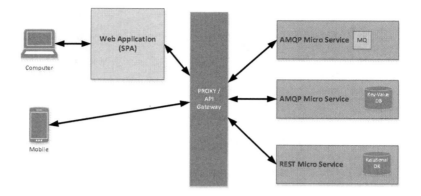

Figure 22 API Gateway

Challenges this pattern solves:

- Granularity of Microservices is often more fine-grained than what a client would need.
- Different clients need different data.
- The numbers and locations of service instances changes dynamically.
- The partitioning of services should be hidden from clients.

Solution:

The API Gateway solves this problem as an entry point for all access to the Microservices. There are several things to keep in mind for requests coming into the API Gateway:

- Proxy/route a single request to a single service instance directly.
- Security could be implemented in the gateway if needed for business needs.

The API Proxy depends on either the Client-side discovery pattern or Server-side discovery pattern to route requests appropriately. (Richardson, 2014)

ORCHESTRATED API PATTERN

The Orchestrated API is a little more complex allowing an API to combine and orchestrate access to many back end services, similar to a service dependency. But there is a clear workflow or orchestration requirement.

The orchestrated API takes generically modeled services and data and prepares them in a more targeted-specific way.

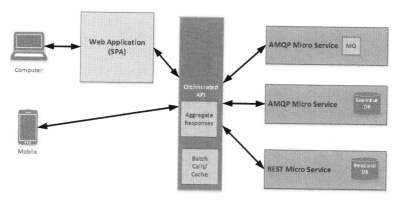

Figure 23 Orchestrated API

CHALLENGES

- Granularity of Microservices is often more fine-grained than what a client would need.
- Different clients need aggregated data.
- The partitioning of services should be hidden from clients.

Solution:

The Orchestrated API solves the aggregation problem and can implement some client-specific needs more possible with the Proxy API pattern.

DISCOVERY PATTERNS

These patterns show how to discover services. The service you want to use needs to be well-known, but the actual logistical details of the specific service instances are what these patterns expose.

CLIENT-SIDE DISCOVERY PATTERN

In Microservices the instances of the services changes dynamically and the location of the services cannot be hardcoded as is done with Monolithic applications. What is needed is a method to dynamically connect to a service whose location is not stable from one moment to the next.

Microservices will expose data using a protocol like REST and have a host and port. The number of services and locations changes dynamically and if hosted in the cloud, the host addresses are also adjusted dynamically.

The client to a service will query a service registry to get the location details of an instance of the service to call.

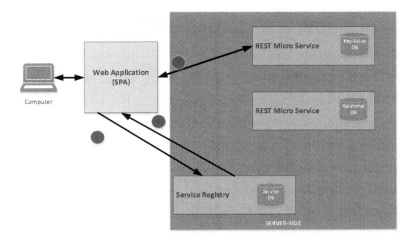

Figure 24 Client-Side Discovery

The logic is outlined below:

1. Client calls service registry to find the service to call.
2. Service Registry returns connection details
3. Client calls the service based on response from the registry.

Benefits:

- Fewer network hops / latency than the server-side discovery pattern.

Drawbacks:

- Client is tightly coupled to a service registry directly.
- Supporting many client architecture can be a challenge also keeping up with the changing

97

client-architecture landscape can be
detrimental.

(Richardson, 2014)

SERVER-SIDE DISCOVERY PATTERN

In Microservices the instances of the services changes
dynamically and the location of the services cannot be
hardcoded like is done with Monolithic applications. What is
needed is a method to dynamically connect to a service
whose location is not stable from one moment to the next.

Microservices will expose data using a protocol like REST
and have a host and port. The number of services and
locations changes dynamically and if hosted in the cloud the
host addresses are also adjusted dynamically.

The client to a service will query a router or gateway, which
in turn will call a service registry to get the location details of
an instance of the service to call. (Richardson, 2014)

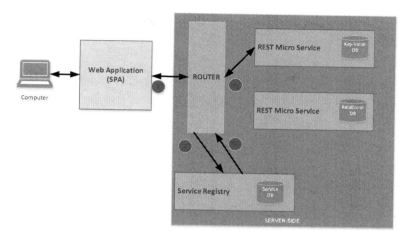

Figure 25 Server-Side Discovery

Benefits:

- Easier to support as the clients do not need to be supported, just the router to the service repository.
- Commonly built into cloud infrastructure.

Drawbacks:

- More network hops / latency than the client-side discovery pattern.
- If not part of a cloud infrastructure it is challenging to build a router and replicate and configure to scale.

REGISTRATION PATTERNS

The service registry pattern is simply a collection of service data in a catalog storing the details of a service, specifically where it is hosted (host, port and version). When a service is started it should be registered and when a service is stopped or crashed it should be deregistered from the registry.

There are two types of registration patterns. One is the self-registration pattern, wherein the services themselves register to be accessible to clients in a dynamic environment. Third-party registration pattern is when a separate system monitors and registers other services with a service registry.

SERVICE REGISTRY PATTERN

The service registry is a catalog or database of services and locations. The registry is populated on service startup with the specific instance details and if a crash or shutdown of a service occurs the registry entry is removed. The registry is used by a client or a router of a Microservice system to find the location of a service or services dynamically. (Richardson, 2014)

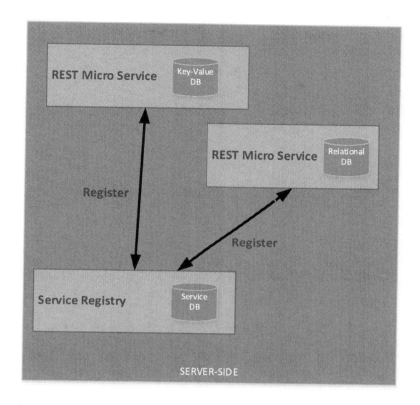

Figure 26 Service Registry

Benefits:

- The registry allows for dynamic discovery of a service instance.

Drawbacks:

- If not part of a cloud infrastructure it is challenging to build a catalog from scratch, with scale, and be managed.

There are two approaches to register with a service registry: self-registration and third-party registration. If a client is accessing a registry, the registry needs to have a fixed address which can be a challenge.

SELF-REGISTRATION PATTERN

When a service starts it needs to register with the registry. When a service is shutdown it needs to be removed from the registry. When a service crashes or is at capacity it needs to be removed from the registry.

For self-registration, the responsibility of the registration and removal from the registry is for the service itself to implement. It is important to renew the registration after a period of time. (Richardson, 2014)

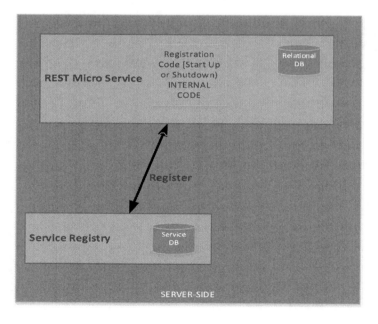

Figure 27 Self-Register

Benefits:

- The service that registers itself knows its own state in more details.

Drawbacks:

- Service registration is programmed in the same language as the service; could be challenging.
- Your service is coupled to the service registry.
- Services cannot detect if they are at capacity easily; there would be a gap in functionality.

THIRD-PARTY REGISTRATION PATTERN

For third-party registration, the responsibility of the registration and removal from the registry is done by a third party component or service. It is important to renew the registration after a period of time. (Richardson, 2014)

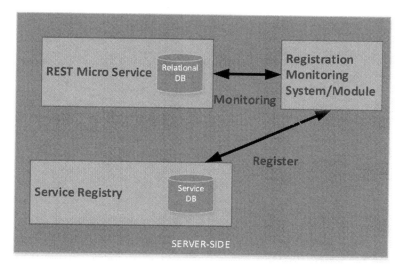

Figure 28 Third Party Registration

103

Benefits:

- The service code is less complex since registration is separated out from the service.
- The registrar can detect health of the service easier and also detect if it is at capacity.

Drawbacks:

- The third-party registrar may not support all features you need like health checks.
- The third-party registrar is not part of existing infrastructure; it is another system that needs to be installed, maintained and configured.

INSTANTIATION PATTERNS

Instantiation patterns are very straightforward. This is how a service is instantiated or created. Below we examine each pattern explaining in detail the benefits and drawbacks.

Challenges for all the instantiation patterns are outlined below:

- Microservices are written on different technology stacks.
- Microservices scale out by leveraging multiple instances per a service.
- Each service is independently scalable and deployable.
- Deployment should be quick.
- Service usage of resources should be configurable.

- Services need to be monitored.

MULTIPLE SERVICE INSTANCES PER HOST PATTERN

Multiple service instances per a host as typically implemented using a language-level virtual machine with:

- Each service instance in a separate language virtual machine.
- Each service instance is shared in a single virtual machine.

These configurations are differentiated on the memory needs and service types as well. (Richardson, 2014)

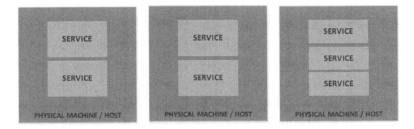

Figure 29 Multiple Instances per Host

Benefits:

- This pattern is more efficient than the service-per host pattern.

Drawbacks:

- Risk of high memory usage.
- Dependencies in JVMs can be a technical challenge.
- Does not control the resource consumption of the service instances.

- If services share a JVM instance there is no isolation or controlled resource consumption.

SINGLE SERVICE INSTANCE PER HOST PATTERN

Single service instances per a host basically has each service instance on its own host or machine. (Richardson, 2014)

Figure 30 Single Service per Host Pattern

Benefits:

- Services are isolated.
- Resource usage and dependencies are contained.

Drawbacks:

- Less efficient than multiple services per host pattern.

SERVICE INSTANCE PER VM PATTERN

Single service instances per a VM basically has each service instance on its own virtual machine image. (Richardson, 2014)

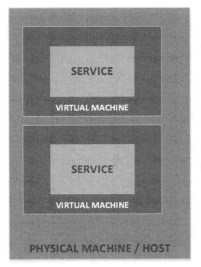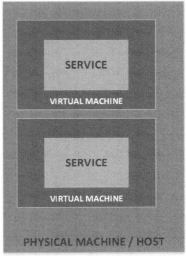

Figure 31 Single Service Instance per VM

Benefits:

- Services are isolated using a more robust technology and are more efficient with resources.
- Supported by many different cloud platforms.
- VMs allow for CPU and resource limitations.

Drawbacks:

- VMs take up more space than containers.
- VMs take more time to setup.

SERVICE INSTANCE PER CONTAINER PATTERN

Single service instances per a container basically has each service instance within its own container. Using Docker, Rocket or Glassware 2.0 a service can be packaged and deployed very easily. (Richardson, 2014)

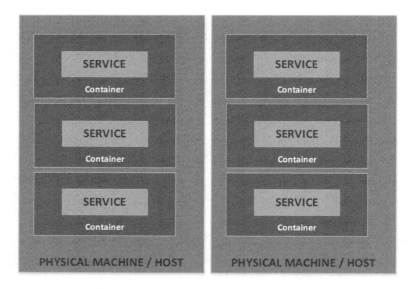

Figure 32 Service Instance per Container

Benefits:

- Scaling is straightforward and predictable.
- Services are isolated.
- Containers limit resource usage.
- Containers are 100x faster than virtual machine images.
- Containers use less memory than virtual machines.

Drawbacks:

- The infrastructure support is not as fully featured as virtual machines.
- Containers are newer technology, thus not as proven as virtual machines
- Containers are more challenging to configure with SSL or other security requirements.

SYSTEM PATTERNS

Higher level system patterns are patterns that are applied at a systems level in a Microservice architecture. With patterns the definition is in the requirements and needs of a system and a pattern should never be implemented without weighing all of the benefits and drawbacks against the context, goals and needs for the business.

This section outlines the common systems patterns used by many Microservice systems. These patterns solve many common problems like communication, data access, cascading failures and availability.

MESSAGE BROKER

The message broker pattern is a standard common systems pattern. How do we keep the complexity of many distributed services from getting out of hand? We do not directly connect the services, but use a Message Broker using events to communicate between the services. Message Broker is a very common pattern using the standard Publish/Subscribe connectivity mechanism.

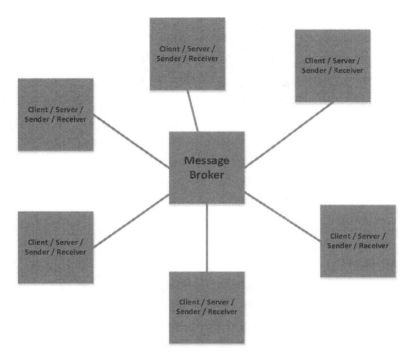

Figure 33 Message Broker

Benefits:

- This pattern decouples services from each other.
- Following this pattern will reduce complexity of the service interactions.
- Allows for some advanced functionality like persistent messages or guarantee the order of messages.

Drawbacks:

- Risk of failure need to have a scalable and reliable messaging system.

110

COMMAND QUERY RESPONSIBILITY SEGREGATION (CQRS)

The command query responsibility segregation pattern is a fancy name for simply separating "reads" from the "writes." Thinking along these lines you can see the value of not having the same services responsible for reading data being the same service that writes the data.

A great example is if an application is performing 90% reads and 10% writes. Writing data is typically more validation intensive and prone to risk (security, access, validation) so separating out that part of the system adds more complexity to an overall system, thus making gains in performance, security and maintenance.

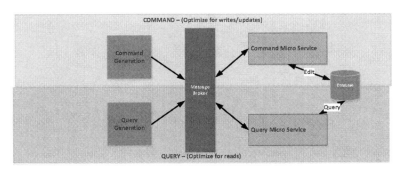

Figure 34 CQRS Pattern

Benefits:

- This pattern decouples read logic from write logic, making system more resilient.
- Following this pattern will show clearly how data access is used by the systems.
- Easier to take a complex system and allow performance to improve.

Drawbacks:

- More complicated interaction pattern.
- Usually implemented using events and some complex interactions for writing and reading at the same time.

TWELVE – FACTOR

The Twelve Factor App (Wiggins, 2012) also known just as Twelve Factor is a methodology for building software delivered as a service. Twelve-Factor was written for building and deploying apps on the Heroku PaaS. Many of these factors are part of the Microservice principles in Chapter 1 and 2. If you are developing applications for the cloud, these twelve factors are like a best-practices for making maintenance and management of the systems best in breed.

THE TWELVE FACTORS

I.   Codebase

        One codebase tracked in revision control, many deploys.

II.   Dependencies
        Explicitly declare and isolate dependencies.

III.   Config
        Store config in the environment.

IV.   Backing Services
        Treat backing services as attached resources.

V.   Build, Release, Run

Strictly separate build and run stages.

VI. Processes
Execute the app as one or more stateless processes.

VII. Port Binding
Export services via port binding.

VIII. Concurrency
Scale out via the process model.

IX. Disposability
Maximize robustness with fast startup and graceful shutdown.

X. Dev/Prod Parity
Keep development, staging and production as similar as possible.

XI. Logs
Treat logs as event streams.

XII. Admin Processes
Run admin/management tasks as one-off processes.

CIRCUIT BREAKER

The circuit breaker in software is exactly what it is in electrical wiring for building. Just like a wiring system, a circuit breaker will detect a broken "service" and disable future calls to that system by bypassing it. A circuit breaker can have more advanced features where the breaker intelligently resets itself. (Nygard, 2007)

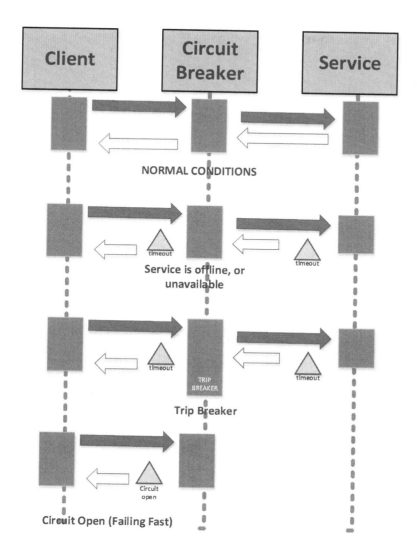

Figure 35 Circuit Breaker Pattern

It is important to note that the circuit breaker should not be used as part of a desired use-case, but as a way from keeping your entire system going offline, providing partial features or success and preventing the long-winded timeout issues. Once a system is known to be offline you should not have to wait very long to figure this out.

BULKHEADS

A bulkhead is a segment in the hull of a ship that if flooded will not result in the ship sinking, thus containing the problem (usually a breach in the hull). In software this is typically the solution we use for availability of critical systems. It is commonly implemented using redundancy, and many times at many different levels. (Nygard, 2007)

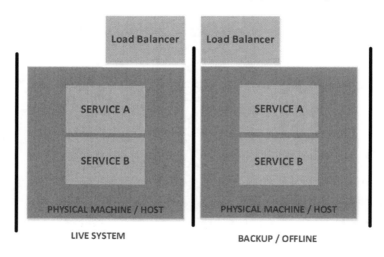

Figure 36 Bulkhead Pattern

How does this apply to Microservices? We can implement bulkhead at many different levels by allocating resources depending on the requirements of our systems. We can apply redundancy at the service level, thread-pool level, router and system level or even higher.

116

As for patterns for Microservices, this one is much more straightforward when using containers as they make redundancy as simple as just instantiating new services. The challenge is in the coordination of the instantiation and reservation of resources for the containers.

SUMMARY

This chapter discussed the patterns useful for the implementation and design of Microservices. We went over the most important API patterns, along with registration, discovery and instantiation patterns. The system patterns are broader and, depending on the needs of the system, approaches specific problems and challenges. Almost all these patterns are standard and are currently used throughout systems. These patterns offer special and specific value to Microservices as they adhere to the principles of Microservices and enable the implementation of the principles. Microservices inherited many of the principles from the Twelve-Factor application methodology.

CHAPTER 12. MAKING YOUR SERVICES SUCCESSFUL

What is the definition of success? Only you can know what you mean by success, but in the context of software design, development and management: success is related to the goals of the software. Successful software embraces these characteristics, so our definitions of success should be in alignment. It is important to know the goals and purposes of the software. If the goals are not similar to these, Microservices is probably not the solution.

- No defects (it does what it should do)
- Meets the needs of the users:
  - ○ Secure.
  - ○ Scalable – software is designed to support large amounts of users.
  - ○ Robust – can withstand failures or unpredictable changes.
- Easy to manage and release.
- Straightforward to change.
- On budget.
- On time.

Depending on your systems needs and challenges, Microservice architecture can aide you in the battle for successful software. It is a real challenge to implement these architectures as they are relatively new to the industry and the technologies are changing rapidly making it difficult to even know where to start to learn the method and concepts. The key principles of Microservices comes to the rescue and the starting point is outlined below.

The first step is assessing the current organizational structure of the development teams and business areas and seeing if there will be a conflict as is explained in Conway's Law.

"Organizations which design systems ... are constrained to produce designs which are copies of the communication structures of these organizations" – (Conway, 1968)

Basically if you try to build services using the Microservices architecture and your teams and business groups do not align organizationally to the service functions and goals, you will be fighting against a current of inertia that will be difficult to overcome.

Some strategies to employ here are if an organization is small enough or new enough to try out new ideas, you can start small with teams aligned in business and development around a logical functional area for some Microservices decomposed from an existing monolithic application.

Try to limit team size to no more than 8 to 12 people as there is a communication overhead with more than that, making the team less efficient. Small services equals small teams.

If the services and releases are proven successful, well and good. But if not, adjust, reassess, refactor and attach again using retrospectives. The goal is to scale this to large and more complex systems where it makes sense. You should not try to force every system into a Microservice architecture if it doesn't make sense based on goals and needs.

The second step, once your team structure and development structure are aligned, is to choose a technology that makes the most sense for the problem-space. If utilizing a document database with node.js services exposing REST API with JSON data then you can go for it. If the technology makes sense for a relational database, TCP/IP service and distributed in-memory databases, you should go for it. This is a real win with Microservices as it can make the team much more productive. One caveat is licensing cost and training issues on some of these choices, which must be acceptable to the team and management. In most cases these costs are far less than picking a misfit technology for a problem space it is not designed for, leading to performance, maintenance, and vendor –lock-in, which can really add up in costs.

The third step is to develop and leverage DevOps using continuous integration, automated testing, appropriate virtualization for hosting services, source control and automated environment deployment, setup and management. Depending on technologies needed and skills of the organization this could take some time to establish. There are many open-source and commercial variants of open-source software with support contracts to lower exposure to the newer technologies.

Setting up service registry, catalog and gateway for service discovery all take time to get right, and you may find many existing solutions that give you the features you need with minimal setup. I have found that by writing my own basic needs first goes a long way in keeping things simple. Depending on your needs you have to weigh the choices and make a decision, but leveraging a cloud platform or DevOps tooling commercial or open-source can get you up to speed and add consists. This will make your life much better in the long run.

The fourth step is once your first feature(s) / services are coded up and hosted in development / testing environments, you will need to push things out to production environment getting things configured and setup. This is the most exciting part as you see the simplicity of the services alongside the complexity of a distributed architecture. Thus you are leveraging the tooling and technology that makes this much easier than in prior years.

The big parts of setting up production is the logging, capacity planning, debug information, and production service statistics (if needed), right off the bat, as well as integration testing with other systems. This is the first time releasing a Microservice within the environment.

The last step is the best – versioning the system according to needs and updating the code to add new features and keep things current. The lessons learned from the first go-around are immense as it is a philosophy and a way of doing business that makes things so much simpler and also makes enterprise development fun. Process review, retrospectives and agile development methodology are critical to the success of the software. Learning and adjusting is the big idea here. Nothing will work perfectly the first time around, but as you learn and adjust, things will fall into place and make sense.

SIMPLICITY

Trying to keep things simple is one of the most difficult skills to master. Patterns have emerged as a way to aid in this. While patterns do not collectively make things simpler, they elevate the discussion through a common language and a common approach to identifying and solving problems. Patterns is the way to progress our understanding of systems, making communication easier and identifying and implementing the solution to a common problem and generally making things more efficient.

Making communication of complicated ideas easier and clearer is the key to generally making the architecture of things simpler. Some of the principles that lead to simplicity are the DRY (Don't Repeat Yourself) (The Pragmatic Programmer: From Journeyman to Master , 1999) and SOLID (Single responsibility, Open-closed, Liskov substitution, Interface segregation and Dependency inversion) approaches. (Martin, 2009)

ORGANIZATIONAL ALIGNMENT

Conway's Law outlines the challenges of an organization not aligned to the development structure. It is fascinating how things that don't appear to be related, are indeed related. No wonder many efficient technology companies implemented feature teams as a way to add features to complex and large systems to great success.

CULTURE

While the culture of a company cannot easily change, it does indeed change. Clearly laying out the goals, principles and definition of success goes a long way to identifying the culture of the company. Once defined, strategies for aligning the culture to those values and principles are more straightforward. A company should have a mission statement as well a common calling and goal. Having principles in common with the Microservices principles is the key to making cultural inertia work to make the technology teams and solutions successful.

What's Next?

With the knowledge from this book explaining the patterns and applications of Microservices to help solve business problems, now the next step is getting started.

The goal of this book was to introduce the patterns, architectures and applications of Microservices, also known as the why, what and how of Microservices, and putting them to work in your organization.

There is a large community of developers, architects and managers who are passionate about solving problems and making the world a better place. You should get involved in your community, share your stories and solutions, ask for help and offer help. We are in this together.

Summary

This final chapter discussed the needs to make your services successful. Nothing is successful without measuring and knowing what success is, and it is different for many systems. Aligning goals and principles are keys to success. Organizational structure impacts code and project structure for long-term success with these technologies and architectures; the organization must embrace this fact. The services will only achieve long term success with the culture and people aligning with the principles for Microservices. Take the knowledge from this book and use it to build and design Microservice Architecture systems.

REFERENCES

(1968). In F. Brooks, *The Mythical Man-Month.* Addison-Wesley.

(1999). In D. T. Andres Hunt, *The Pragmatic Programmer: From Journeyman to Master* . The Pragmatic Programmers, LLC.

Conway, M. E. (1968). How do Committees Invent? *Datamation*, 28-31.

Einstein, A. (1933). On the Method of Theoretical Physics. *Philosophy of Science.*

Fowler, M., & Lewis, J. (2014, March 25). *Microservices.* Retrieved from MartinFowler.com: http://martinfowler.com/articles/microservices.html

Martin, R. C. (2009). *Getting a SOLID start.* Retrieved from https://sites.google.com/site/unclebobconsultingllc/getting-a-solid-start

Nygard, M. T. (2007). *Release It!: Design and Deploy Production-Ready Software.* Pragmatic Bookshelf.

Raymond, E. S. (2003). *The Art of UNIX Programming.* Addison-Wesley .

Richardson, C. (2014, March 18). *Microservice architecture patterns and best practices.* Retrieved from Microservices.IO: http://microservices.io/

Wiggins, A. (2012, 1 30). Retrieved from The Twelve Factor App: http://12factor.net/

ABOUT THE AUTHOR

 **Lucas Krause** is an entrepreneur, consultant, software developer and architect. He started building programs when he was only eight years old with his parents' Commodore 64. Lucas studied electrical engineering in college and fell in love with hardware and software technology focused solutions.

Lucas is fortunate to work on a variety of projects large and complex project with small or large teams, always making big impacts and making the project a success. A man wearing many hats

Lucas has designed, built, lead, and delivered over 100 successful projects in over a dozen different industries. Lucas's passion is solving customer's problems long-term leading to sustainable growth and success. Lucas enjoys educating and inspiring others to learn from his experience in solving their own problems and making the world a better place.

Learn more about Lucas at:

http://www.amazon.com/author/lucaskrause